C000067265

LOTHIAN BUSES

BUSES

AN ERA OF CHANGE IN EDINBURGH

Front Cover: Volvo 7900H hybrid 37/BG64 FXM bears the latest corporate design and livery whilst parked outside Annandale Street garage as dawn breaks over Edinburgh on 18 July 2019.

Rear Cover: Volvo B5TL 495/SF17 VOJ, with Wrightbus Gemini 3 bodywork, displays the Edinburgh Zoo Giraffe advertising livery as it operates a Route 26 Tranent–Clerwood service whilst traversing Princes Street on 21 August 2021.

LOTHIAN BUSES

BUSES

AN ERA OF CHANGE IN EDINBURGH

FRED KERR

PEN & SWORD
TRANSPORT

AN IMPRINT OF PEN & SWORD BOOKS LTD.
YORKSHIRE – PHILADELPHIA

First published in Great Britain in 2024 by
Pen and Sword Transport
An imprint of
Pen & Sword Books Ltd.
Yorkshire - Philadelphia

ISBN 978 1 39905 434 8

Typeset in 10/12 Palatino by SJmagic DESIGN SERVICES, India.

Printed and bound in India by Replika Press Pvt. Ltd.

Pen & Sword Books Ltd incorporates the imprints of Pen & Sword Books Archaeology, Atlas, Aviation, Battleground, Discovery, Family History, History, Maritime, Military, Naval, Politics, Railways, Select, Transport, True Crime, Fiction, Frontline Books, Leo Cooper, Praetorian Press, Seaforth Publishing, Wharncliffe and White Owl.

For a complete list of Pen & Sword titles please contact

PEN & SWORD BOOKS LIMITED
George House, Units 12 & 13, Beevor Street, Off Pontefract Road,
Barnsley, South Yorkshire, S71 1HN, England
E-mail: enquiries@pen-and-sword.co.uk
Website: www.pen-and-sword.co.uk

or

PEN AND SWORD BOOKS
1950 Lawrence Rd, Havertown, PA 19083, USA
E-mail: uspen-and-sword@casematepublishers.com
Website: www.penandswordbooks.com

CONTENTS

INTRODUCTION

L othian Buses can trace its beginnings back to 1919 when the City Corporation of Edinburgh took over the Edinburgh & District Tramway company when the lease of the latter company ended on 30 June 1919 and created the Edinburgh City Tramways Department (ECT) company to run it. In parallel with the take-over, it introduced a seasonal bus touring service around Holyrood Park using Leyland vehicles. The use of buses continued as the ECT decided to convert the cable tramway to an electric tramway to improve connectivity with the electric tramway system of both Leith and Portobello, districts which were absorbed into Edinburgh during the early 1920s. The bus operations expanded quickly as an initial plan was to replace the ECT cable network by bus operation rather than convert it to electric traction but by 1925 it was decided to operate trams for the heaviest and busiest routes whilst the bus operation, originally providing replacement services during the changeover, was directed to routes complementing existing tram routes and providing services to new districts more quickly than tramways as the city expanded its boundaries.

In 1928, the growing importance of buses to the transport network led Edinburgh City Tramways to be renamed as Edinburgh Corporation Transport (ECT) and the bus and tramway routes were run to complement each other in the provision of Edinburgh's transport. When the decision was taken in the 1950s to replace the tramway network by buses, 300 Leyland buses were ordered over a 4-year period, supported by smaller deliveries of 100 Guy Arab buses including 50 re-bodied from the ex-London Transport fleet. This changeover, with its concentration on Leyland vehicles, resulted in ECT becoming a loyal customer for Leyland, thus simplifying spares and maintenance until the company's demise in 1988.

ECT continued operating until 1975, when local government re-organisation imposed legal restrictions that banned the city from direct involvement in public transport, hence a new body, Lothian Region Transport (LRT), was created as a commercial company by Edinburgh City Council (with 91 per cent of shares) in alliance with Midlothian Council (with 5 per cent of shares), East Lothian Council (with 3 per cent of shares) and West Lothian Council (with 1 per cent of shares); the new company began operating on 16 May 1975. The company has proved commercially successful, making regular annual profits whilst expanding its range of services leading to it being re-named Lothian Buses (LB) in January 2000.

The company continues to innovate with its routes which are subject to regular review whilst remaining loyal to its suppliers. Following the changeover from tramway to bus operation in the 1950s, ECT remained a loyal Leyland customer until the company suffered financial problems in the 1980s, resulting in it being sold to Volvo Bus in 1988. This led LRT to purchase a number of Dennis vehicles but in 2001 purchases of Volvo vehicles heralded a new era of supplier loyalty that continues through to the present day. Edinburgh has also shown loyalty to its bodywork suppliers, initially with Alexanders of Falkirk then the Volvo/Wrightbus partnership but, following Wrightbus entering administration in September 2019, Volvo has returned to Alexanders (now trading as Alexander Dennis) for Lothian Buses vehicles.

Lothian Buses has committed to reaching zero carbon emissions by 2030, hence recent developments by the company have included the provision of test facilities for a range of innovations including electric vehicles and the development of new vehicle designs with suppliers whilst also creating new companies to maintain services from outside the city boundary and initiating a new tramway network connecting Edinburgh city centre with the airport (see Sections 3 and 5).

I have been interested in the city's transport since experiencing the tram-to-bus changeover in the 1950s. I moved south to England with my parents in 1956 shortly before the final tram operation in November 1956 but retained an interest in the city's transport network. Over time, I have made many visits to Edinburgh to visit relatives and have noted the changes, including the fact that after 15 years' daily service, Edinburgh's buses are highly valued in the second-hand market. I finally undertook to record these changes in 2011 when my experience of digital photography encouraged me to photograph the current fleet during my irregular visits, thus providing sufficient material to compile this album of record. Section 1 notes changes within the city fleet whilst Section 3 notes changes in the Lothian Buses-owned companies which operate outside the city boundary as the company seeks to achieve zero carbon emissions by 2030.

This album thus shows my impression of the changes that I have noted in the period between 2011 and 2022 and hopefully confirms Lothian Buses to be one of the most successful municipal bus operations within Scotland - if not within the United Kingdom.

SECTION 1:
CITY SERVICES

1.1: PRINCES STREET

Princes Street is Edinburgh's main thoroughfare which begins at its eastern end as the continuation of the A1 London–Edinburgh trunk route then continues for 1.2km (0.75 miles) to its western end where it becomes the A8 Edinburgh–Glasgow trunk route. Princes Street was part of the New Town created in the eighteenth century and, following concerns at its original name (St Giles Street) being expressed by King George III, the name Princes Street was suggested and approved.

Initially built from 1770 as a residential area on its northern edge, the properties were converted to retail use during the nineteenth century whilst the gardens on the southern edge were developed after the draining of the Nor' Loch, following rejection of an earlier proposal to extend the loch to Leith and provide a direct marine link to the Firth of Forth which provides the northern boundary of the city.

As the main thoroughfare, Princes Street sees an estimated 400 public service vehicles traverse it per hour; many are services operated by Lothian Buses, most of whose routes pass along part, if not all, its length. Sightings of the Lothian Buses fleet between 2011 and 2022 have noted three corporate liveries borne by the vehicles; the earliest livery was defined as the Harlequin livery which was initially applied to identify low-floor vehicles supplied by Dennis between 1999-2004 before being adopted as the corporate livery for the fleet. This changed in 2013, after Lothian Buses withdrew its last high-step vehicles in 2010, when the company adopted the Flowline design applied to its ADL Enviro 400 vehicles (fleet numbers 201–215) whilst replacing the madder and dark cream colours with madder and white. In 2016, the introduction of a batch of Volvo B5TL vehicles saw the Flowline design replaced by a more angular design that is, as at 2022, being applied to both the city fleets and those of the associated East Coast Buses' and Lothian Country Buses' fleets (see Section 3). Initially the angular design had sharp corners but these were subsequently made round to soften the appearance of the design.

(Image 1): Volvo B7TL 751/SN56 AAE, with Wrightbus Gemini 1 bodywork, displays the Flowline design in the favoured madder/white colours as it passes the Sir Walter Scott monument whilst working from Silverknowes to Colinton on 17 April 2017 and is overtaken by Volvo B9TL 921/SN08 BYP, with Wrightbus Gemini 1 bodywork also bearing the Flowline design in madder/white as it works from Wallyford to Balerno.

(Image 2): Volvo B9TL 393/SN11 EEF, with Wrightbus Gemini 3 bodywork, works from Hillend to The Jewel on 10 April 2018 as Volvo B7TL 745/SN55 BOU, with Wrightbus Gemini 1 bodywork, turns onto Frederick Street whilst working from Riccarton to Restalrig.

(Image 3): On 12 April 2019, two different operators were noted using Volvo B5TL vehicles with Wrightbus Gemini 3 bodywork. Vehicle 492/SF17 VOD displays the angular design and madder and white colours whilst working from Clerwood to Tranent as it overtakes vehicle 510/SF17 VPL working an Airlink Airport–Waverley Bridge service.

1.2: SINGLE DECK VEHICLES

Many of the routes within Edinburgh passed under low bridges, hence ECT operated a large number of single deck vehicles on various routes over the years. Whilst some progress has been made to lower roads to allow the use of double deck vehicles, the single deck vehicles still find favour with Lothian Buses as the current operator of the city's transport services.

1.2.1: FLEET NUMBER 51–100
Dennis/Transbus Dart SLF with Plaxton Pointer bodywork

This fleet was delivered between November 2002 and October 2003 as part of the move to low-floor buses, but the Dennis vehicles were soon replaced by deliveries of Volvo B7RLE vehicles with Wrightbus Eclipse bodywork. When withdrawn from service many were sold on to other operators throughout the UK for further service.

(Image 4): Vehicle 75/SN53 JNO, bearing Flowline design with madder/white colours, passes Princes St East Gardens on 15 September 2014 whilst working from Seafield to the Gyle Centre during its final days of operation with Lothian Buses.

(Image 5): Vehicle 88/SN53 AUY bears the Harlequin livery as it passes along Princes Street on 20 August 2011 whilst working an Easter Road–Clermiston service. This is a traditional single deck vehicle service because the route encompasses many low bridges that are considered too low for double deck vehicles.

(Image 6): When withdrawn from service, vehicle 53/SK52 OHW was retained for use as a driver training vehicle and re-numbered TB (Training Bus) 53, on which duty it was noted passing along Princes Street on 29 June 2015.

1.2.2: FLEET NUMBER 101–166
Volvo B7RLE with Wrightbus Eclipse Urban bodywork

This fleet was delivered in five batches; 101–130 in March 2004, 131–135 in September 2005, 136–150 in March 2007, 151–160 in September 2007 and 161–166 in September 2008. This fleet was ordered as part of the decision to commit to Volvo vehicles which replaced the earlier Dennis Dart fleet (see Section 1.2.1).

The original Harlequin livery was exchanged in 2010 for a return to Edinburgh's traditional madder and white colours displayed in a Flowline style.

(Image 7): Vehicle 140/SK07 CGY stops outside the Princes Street branch of British Home Stores on 29 June 2015 whilst working from Clovenstone to Musselburgh.

(Image 8): Vehicle 145/SK07 CFX approaches the Waverley Bridge traffic lights on 15 September 2014 whilst working from Gilmerton to Silverknowes. Note the orange roof which was part of a route identification system in which orange denoted Route 29 serving the Silverknowes to Gorebridge route, designated the 'Stock Brig' route, or any part thereof.

Above (Image 9):
Vehicle 159/SN57 DDE
passes along Princes
Street on 29 June
2015 whilst working
a Waverley Bridge–
Davidson's Mains service.

Left (Image 10): Vehicle
159/SN57 DDE departs
from Gyle Centre on
28 May 2018 while
working a service to
The Jewel.

(Image 11): Following
withdrawal from service,
vehicle 102/SN04 NGE was
adapted for continued use
as a driver training vehicle
in which role it was noted
passing along Princes Street
on 29 June 2015.

(Image 12): Vehicle 134/SN55 BJU traverses the Hanover Street/The Mound intersection of Princes Street on 11 September 2015 whilst working a Holyrood Circular service that started from Hanover Street. This unusual intersection of Princes Street is one which is operated as a through route, with traffic banned from turning onto, or joining from, Princes Street.

(Image 13): In 2016, the delivery of a batch of Volvo B5TL vehicles introduced a more angular design which was adopted as the latest company style and was applied retrospectively to the whole fleet. Vehicle 136/SK07 CGO displays the new style on 12 April 2019 as it calls at Edinburgh Parkway, adjacent to Hermiston Gate, whilst working from the Ocean Terminal to the Gyle Centre with a service that avoided the city centre and Princes Street – one of the few services to do so.

(Image 14): After withdrawal from city service, vehicle 103/SN04 NGF was retained and adapted for driver training by receiving yellow livery and re-numbering to TB (Training Bus) 103, in which guise it was noted passing along Princes Street on 4 March 2020 with a trainee driver in the driving seat.

1.2.3: FLEET NUMBER 167–190; 193–199
Volvo B7RLE with Wrightbus Eclipse 2 bodywork

This fleet was a follow-on order from the earlier series (see Section 1.2.2) to release the Dennis/Transbus Dart SLF vehicles as part of a transfer to Volvo vehicles and was delivered in five batches between February 2009 and May 2013; 167–170 in February 2009, 171–175 in December 2012, 176–190 in May 2013 and 195–199 in October 2012 whilst 193/4 were bought from Whitelaw's Coaches, Stonehouse in 2011. Many vehicles from this batch were subsequently transferred to Lothian Country Buses when that company was created to take up East Lothian services that were surrendered by the First Group operator (see Section 3). The East Lothian services were subsequently re-formed into East Coast Buses and the Lothian Country Buses name was later resuscitated to operate services that were surrendered within West Lothian (see Section 3).

Left (Image 15): Vehicle 174/SN60 EOG approaches Princes Street from North Bridge on 10 April 2018 whilst working from Rosewell to Fort Kinnaird.

Below (Image 16): Vehicle 172/SN60 EOE traverses the Hanover Street/The Mound intersection of Princes Street on 10 April 2018 whilst working from Craigleith to King's Road.

(Image 17): Vehicle 171/SN60 EOD approaches Princes Street from Frederick Street whilst in use as a driver training vehicle on 5 May 2022.

(Image 18): Vehicle 178/SN13 BEO passes Princes Street Gardens on 15 September 2014 whilst working from Seafield to the Gyle Centre.

(Image 19): Vehicle 170/SN58 BYX approaches Princes Street from North Bridge on 10 April 2018 whilst working from Riccarton to Queen Margaret University.

(Image 20): Vehicle 187/SN13 BFM turns out of South St David Street onto Princes Street on 31 July 2018 whilst working from Seafield to Broomhouse (part of the route).

(Image 21): Vehicle TB (Training Bus) 107/RIG 6498 approaches Princes Street East Gardens on 4 March 2020 whilst being driven by a trainee driver under instruction. This vehicle was originally registered as SF55 HHC and was initially bought by Whitelaw's Coaches of Stenhouse in November 2005. The vehicle was bought by Lothian Buses in 2011 to become fleet number 193 before transfer to East Coast Buses in 2016 where it was re-numbered fleet number 10193 and re-registered with its current registration.

(Image 22): Following withdrawal from service, vehicle 167/SN58 BYU was adapted for driver training and renumbered Fleet Number TB (Training Bus)1. On 10 April 2018 it was noted turning from Frederick Street onto Princes Street with a trainee in the driving seat.

1.2.4: FLEET NUMBER 278–283
Optare M960 with Optare Solo SR bodywork

This small fleet was bought in 2008 on behalf of Mac Tours, a private company which had begun operating tours of Edinburgh in 1998; the company was bought by Lothian Buses in 2002 but continued operating under its original name. The fleet was initially allocated Fleet Numbers 35–40 but was renumbered to 278–283 when the order for Volvo 7900H vehicles was placed (see Section 1.2.5). The fleet was replaced in turn by the delivery of Wrightbus Street Air vehicles (see Section 1.2.6) and sold on to other UK operators.

Above (Image 23): Vehicle 281/SN08 BZA turns out of Frederick Street onto Princes Street on 24 June 2015 whilst working the West End Circular service.

Left (Image 24): Vehicle 281/SN08 BZA passes along Princes Street on 10 April 2018 whilst working on a West End Circular service.

1.2.5: FLEET NUMBER 1–50
Volvo 7900H Hybrid with Volvo bodywork

The initial fleet of ten vehicles was delivered in March 2013 with three subsequent batches being delivered up to September 2014; 11–30 between May and July 2014, 31–38 between November and December 2014 and 39–50 between November and December 2014. Their first appearances were on the Route 1 Easter Road–Clermiston service but over time the vehicles have also moved onto other single deck vehicle routes including Route 30 Clovenstone–Musselburgh and Route 12 to the Gyle Centre services. The latter service has had various start points as the city services have changed to meet new passenger demands.

This fleet was an early introduction to the Lothian operator of electric vehicles, hence the madder/dark cream colouring that was used to highlight the fact to the travelling public. When Lothian buses had withdrawn the last of its step buses in 2010 to operate all low-floor vehicles, the Harlequin livery was replaced by this fleet's livery, albeit with white instead of dark cream as the operator reverted to its traditional madder and white colour scheme when adopting the Flowline design. In 2016 the introduction of a batch of Volvo B5TL vehicles with Wrightbus Gemini 3 bodywork (Fleet Numbers 441–465 – see Section 1.3.8) saw a further change as the Flowline design was replaced by a more angular design that was subsequently adopted as the new corporate livery.

(Image 25): Vehicle 35/BG64 FXJ passes Princes Street Gardens on 30 June 2015 whilst working from Easter Road to Clermiston.

(Image 26): Vehicle 17/BT14 DKE calls at a Princes Street bus-stop on 28 October 2017 whilst working from Clovenstone to Musselburgh.

Opposite (Image 27): Vehicle 1/LB13 BUS approaches Waverley Bridge traffic lights on 24 June 2015 whilst working from Easter Road to Clermiston.

Above (Image 28): Vehicle 18/BT14 DKF collects passengers from outside the British Home Stores on 11 September 2015 whilst working from Clovenstone to Musselburgh.

Left (Image 29): Vehicle 21/BT14 DKL halts outside Princes Street Gardens on 12 April 2019 whilst working from Musselburgh to Clovenstone.

(Image 30): Vehicle 41/BT64 LHW turns out of South St David Street onto Princes Street on 24 June 2015 whilst working from Seafield to the Gyle Centre.

(Image 31): Vehicle 6/SN13 BDO turns out of Lothian Road onto Princes Street on 29 June 2015 whilst working from Clermiston to Easter Road.

(Image 32): Vehicle 3/SN13 BCY, working from Easter Road to Clermiston on 29 June 2015, overtakes sister vehicle 45/BT64 LJA as the latter halts at the bus stop adjacent to Princes Street East Gardens whilst working from Seafield to the Gyle Centre.

(Image 33): Dawn breaks over Edinburgh on 19 July 2019 as vehicle 37/BG64 FXM, bearing the latest angular design of madder/white livery, is parked outside Annandale Street garage, both the main garage and headquarters of Lothian Buses, awaiting its duties for the day.

Right (Image 34): Vehicle 29/BT14 DLE passes South St David Street on 18 July 2019 whilst working from Clovenstone to Musselburgh.

Below (Image 35): Vehicle 2/HY13 BUS turns out of South St David Street onto Princes Street on 5 May 2022 whilst working from Seafield to the Gyle Centre.

(Image 36): Vehicle 1/LB13 BUS pulls away from the bus-stop outside Princes Street East Gardens on 21 August 2021 whilst working from Seafield to the Gyle Centre.

(Image 37): Vehicle 27/BT14 DKY passes Princes Street Gardens on 12 April 2019 whilst working from Musselburgh to Clovenstone.

1.2.6: FLEET NUMBER 284–289
Wrightbus StreetAir (Electric) with Wrightbus bodywork

These fully electric vehicles were delivered in October 2017 for trial as Lothian Buses seeks to reduce carbon emissions to zero by 2030. The experience of operation, however, has not met expectations and the subsequent entry of Wrightbus into administration during 2021 means that expected future orders will not be placed. In fact, the fleet was temporarily taken out of service during 2022 and, whilst Wrightbus was bought out of administration, the new owners are intending to concentrate on hydrogen-powered vehicles, which Lothian Buses were yet to trial as at September 2022.

Left (Image 38):
Vehicle 284/SK67 FLC passes along Princes Street on 10 April 2018 whilst working from Clermiston to Easter Road.

Below (Image 39):
Vehicle 287/SK67 FLF turns from Princes Street onto Frederick Street on 12 April 2019 whilst returning to Annandale Street garage at the end of its tour of service.

A vist to Edinburgh on 12 April 2019 at the Frederick Street junction with Princes Street noted ...

Left (Image 40): ... vehicle 285/SK67 FLD turning onto Princess Street from Frederick Street whilst working from West Granton to the Royal Infirmary.

Right (Image 41): ... vehicle 287/SK67 FLF approaching Princes Street from Frederick Street whilst working a West End Circular service.

Below (Image 42): Vehicle 287/ SK67 FLF traverses the Hanover Street/ The Mound intersection of Princes Street on 28 October 2017 whilst working a Holyrood Circular service that begins in Hanover Street.

1.2.7: FLEET NUMBER 66–95
Volvo B8RLE with MCV eVoRa bodywork
This fleet was delivered during January 2021 and vehicles are initially being operated on the Clovenstone–Musselburgh service in conjunction with the Volvo 7900H hybrid vehicles (see Section 1.2.5).

(Image 43): Diverted by bridge maintenance works on North Bridge, vehicle 87/SJ70 HNZ approaches Princes Street from Frederick Street on 5 May 2022 whilst working from Musselburgh to Clovenstone.

(Image 44): Vehicle 79/SJ70 HNP passes the Hanover Street / The Mound intersection of Princes Street on 21 August 2021 whilst working from Clovenstone to Musselburgh.

A visit to Edinburgh on 21 August 2021 noted vehicles passing the Hanover Street / The Mound intersection of Princes Street whilst working Clovenstone to Musselburgh services that included …

(Image 45): … vehicle 81/ SJ70 HNT and …

(Image 46): … vehicle 76/SJ70 HNM and …

(Image 47): … vehicle 73/SJ70 HNH.

1.3: DOUBLE DECK VEHICLES

Whilst ECT operated a large number of single deck vehicles, it also operated a larger number of double deck vehicles. Immediately after the Second World War, it operated a mix of Daimler, Guy and Leyland vehicles but the bulk of the tram replacement orders in the 1950s were gained by Leyland and the operator remained faithful to the company until 1999, when a fleet of Dennis low-floor vehicles was purchased. This was the operator's first step into low-floor buses with orders being given to Dennis as a leading builder of such vehicles. When Volvo, which had bought Leyland Buses in 1988, in conjunction with the Irish firm of Wrightbus, also offered low-floor vehicles, Lothian Buses returned to Volvo as its main vehicle supplier (see Section 1.3.2) and, as at 2022, continues to be a loyal Volvo customer.

1.3.1: FLEET NUMBER 501–706
Dennis/Transbus Trident SLF with bodywork supplied by Alexander, Plaxton and Transbus.

This fleet was delivered in eight batches; 501–510 with Alexander bodywork between May 1999 and July 1999, 511–545 with Plaxton bodywork between October 1999 and November 1999, 546–577 with Plaxton bodywork between June 2000 and August 2000, 578–598 with Plaxton bodywork in October 2000, 599–627 with Plaxton bodywork between September 2001 and November 2001, 635–656 with Plaxton bodywork between November 2002 and December 2002, 657–661 with Plaxton bodywork in September 2003 and 662–706 with Transbus (previously Dennis) bodywork between March 2004 and June 2004. These were the first low-floor vehicles ordered by the company and a Harlequin style livery was adopted to identify this. The fleet was replaced from 2005 by Volvo vehicles with Wrightbus Gemini bodywork.

In 2005 the fleet was subject to renumbering when:

  (i) original batch 657–661 were renumbered to 629–633.
 (ii) vehicle 666 was renumbered to 628.
(iii) vehicles 701–706 were renumbered to 666, 657–661 respectively.

After withdrawal from city service, vehicles 501–530 were converted to open-top vehicles and re-furbished for use as Edinburgh Tour vehicles (see Section 2).

(Image 48): Vehicle 654/SK52 OHR displays the Harlequin livery, applied to denote a low-floor vehicle, as it passes Princes Street Gardens on 15 September 2014 whilst working from Restalrig to Riccarton.

The South St David Street junction with Princess Street sees a large number of movements including ...

(Image 49): ... vehicle 637/SK52 OGV on 20 August 2011 whilst working from the Ocean Terminal to Riccarton.

(Image 50): ... vehicle 645/SK52 OHD on 24 June 2015 whilst en route to start its tour of duty.

Left (Image 51): Vehicle 679/SN04 ACV passes the Sir Walter Scott Monument during its brief passage of Princes Street on 5 August 2015 whilst working from King's Road to Granton.

Right (Image 52): Vehicle 628/SN04 AAU, initially introduced to service as Fleet Number 666, passes the famed Jenners department store at the corner of South St David Street on 30 June 2015 whilst working from Riccarton to the Ocean Terminal.

Below (Image 53): Vehicle 602/SN51 AXG passes Princes Street East Gardens on a wet 15 September 2014 whilst working from Prestonpans to Penicuik.

(Image 54): Vehicle 635/SK52 OGT crosses St Andrews Square on 26 November 2016 whilst working from Silverknowes to Colinton. This was one of two vehicles transferred to Lothian Country Buses shortly after this image was taken when the latter company was created initially to provide East Lothian services surrended by First Group.

(Image 55): Vehicle 639/SK52 OGX turns out of Lothian Road onto Princes Street on 29 June 2015 whilst working from Riccarton to the Ocean Terminal.

(Image 56): Vehicle 653/SK52 OHP turns out of South St David Street onto Princes Street on 24 June 2015 whilst working from Wallyford to Balerno.

(Image 57): Vehicle 599/SN51 AYO passes Princes Street East Gardens on 15 September 2014 whilst working from King's Road to Granton in dire weather conditions.

1.3.2: FLEET NUMBER 701–825
Volvo B7TL with Wrightbus Gemini 1 bodywork

This fleet was delivered in two batches following a move of chassis supplier from Dennis to Volvo with 701–750 delivered between September and December 2005 and 751–825 delivered between November 2006 and February 2007.

A major bus-stop on Princes Street is that adjacent to Princes Street East Gardens where, on 29 June 2015, …

Right (Image 58): … vehicle 701/SN55 BJX was noted pulling away whilst working from Restalrig to Riccarton.

Below (Image 59): … vehicle 722/SN55 BLZ was noted pulling away whilst working from Mayfield to Clovenstone.

Above (Image 60): Vehicle 706/ SN55 BKE approaches South St David Street junction with Princes Street on 24 June 2015 and passes Jenners department store (a famous Edinburgh landmark) whilst working from Riccarton to Restalrig.

Left (Image 61): Vehicle 723/ SN55 BMO leaves Princes Street as it approaches Shandwick Place on 29 June 2015 whilst working from Wallyford to Balerno.

(Image 62): Vehicle 724/SN55 BMU turns out of South St David Street onto Princes Street on 11 September 2015 whilst working from Wallyford to Balerno.

(Image 63): Vehicle 757/SN56 AAV traverses the Hanover Street/The Mound intersection of Princes Street on 28 October 2017 whilst working from Cramond to King's Buildings.

(Image 64): Vehicle 737/SN55 BNU pulls away from a bus-stop outside Princes Street East Gardens on 29 June 2015 whilst working from Restalrig to Riccarton.

(Image 65): Vehicle 811/SN56 AGO carries Poppy Appeal livery on 5 August 2015 as it passes Princes Street Gardens whilst working from Silverknowes to Colinton.

Right (Image 66): Vehicle 792/SN56 AEP traverses the Hanover Street/The Mound intersection of Princes Street on 12 April 2019 whilst working from Cramond to King's Buildings.

Below (Image 67): Vehicle 748/SN55 BPF turns out of South St David Street onto Princes Street on 24 June 2015 whilst working from Wallyford to Balerno.

(Image 68): Vehicle 713/SN55 BKV passes the Balmoral Hotel (previously the North British Hotel) on a wet 15 September 2014 as it prepares to turn right from Princes Street onto North Bridge whilst working from Clovenstone to Mayfield.

(Image 69): Vehicle 708/SN55 BKG pulls away from a bus-stop outside Princes Street East Gardens on 29 June 2015 whilst working from Restalrig to Riccarton.

1.3.3: FLEET NUMBER 985–999
Scania CN94UD with Scania OmniCity bodywork

This fleet was delivered in two batches; 995–999 in August 2006 then 985–994 in September 2007. They were initially allocated to Airlink 100 services before being transferred to city services after three years. In their final years of city services, they continued to serve the Airport by working the Ocean Terminal–Airport service – one of the few which did not pass along Princes Street.

(Image 70): Vehicle 986/ SN57 DAO stands by Tron Kirk on 5 August 2015 as it waits to turn from South Bridge onto High Street, part of the Royal Mile which connects Edinburgh Castle to the Palace of Holyrood, whilst working an Airport – Ocean Terminal service that avoids Princes Street by being routed through the Old Town. This service was later one that became one of the Skylink group of services (see Section 2).

(Image 71): Vehicle 986/SN57 DAO approaches the Gyle Centre on 22 July 2016 whilst working an Airport – Ocean Terminal service that avoids Princes Street by being routed through the Old Town.

1.3.4: FLEET NUMBER 826–925
Volvo B9TL with Wrightbus Gemini 1 bodywork
This fleet was delivered in two batches as a follow up to the initial order for 701–750 with 826–875 delivered between August and November 2007 and 876–925 delivered between June and August 2008.

(Image 72): Vehicle 832/SK07 CBF halts outside the Balmoral Hotel (previously the North British Hotel) on 15 September 2014 as it prepares to turn from Princes Street onto North Bridge whilst working from East Craigs to Polton Mill.

(Image 73): Vehicle 845/SN57 DDV turns out of Frederick Street onto Princes Street on 10 April 2018 whilst working from Silverknowes to Gorebridge.

The fleet was delivered in the Harlequin livery, which was the corporate livery when noted during a visit to Edinburgh on 20 August 2011.

(Image 74): Vehicle 839/ SK07 CCD approaches Princes Street from Waverley Bridge whilst working from King's Buildings to Cramond.

(Image 75): Vehicle 847/SN57 DDY turns onto Princes Street from South St David Street whilst working from Silverknowes to Colinton.

(Image 76): Vehicle 868/SN57 GMX turns from South St David Street onto Princes Street whilst working from the Ocean Terminal to Hyvots Bank.

(Image 77): Vehicle 855/SN57 DFG passes the Waverley Station entrance when crossing Waverley Bridge whilst working from Cramond to King's Buildings.

(Image 78): Vehicle 869/SN57 GMY turns from Princes Street onto South St David Street whilst working from the Royal Infirmary to Muirhouse.

The Harlequin livery was replaced from 2013 by the Flowline livery, a style first introduced on new deliveries of ADL Enviro 400 vehicles.

(Image 79): Vehicle 827/ SK07 CAE turns onto Princes Street from South St David Street on 24 June 2015 whilst working from the Ocean Terminal to Hyvots Bank.

(Image 80): Vehicle 865/ SN57 GMO passes the Hannover Street/The Mound intersection of Princes Street on 24 June 2015 whilst working from Silverknowes to Colinton.

(Image 81): Vehicle 867/ SN57 GMV turns off Princes Street onto South St David Street on 18 July 2019 whilst working from Balerno to Wallyford.

(Image 82): Vehicle 850/SN57 DFA passes along Princes Street on 29 June 2015 whilst working from the Ocean Terminal to Hyvots Bank.

(Image 83): Vehicle 905/SN08 BXY pulls away from the bus-stop outside Princes Street East Gardens on 29 June 2015 whilst working from Gorebridge to Baberton.

Some fleet members carry a dedicated livery promoting a business/charity which is normally retained for a year once released to service.

(Image 84): Vehicle 856/SN57 DFJ bears Breast Cancer Awareness advertising as it calls at a bus-stop adjacent to Princes Street Gardens on 11 September 2015 whilst working from Polton Mill to East Craigs.

(Image 85): Vehicle 901/SN08 BXP bears Lothian Buses advertising as it traverses Princes Street on 11 September 2015 whilst working from Baberton to Gorebridge.

(Image 86): Vehicle 856/SN57 DFJ bears Macmillan Nurses advertising on 28 October 2017 as it prepares to turn off Princes Street onto Frederick Street whilst working from the Royal Infirmary to Muirhouse.

(Image 87): Vehicle 851/SN57 DFC passes Princes Street East Gardens on 28 October 2017 whilst working a special service from St Andrews Square to Ingliston Showground dedicated to the Elrow Music Festival.

In 2016 the Flowline design was replaced by the Angular design, initially introduced with deliveries of Volvo B5TL vehicles.

(Image 88): Vehicle 827/SK07 CAE approaches the Hanover Street / The Mound intersection of Princes Street on 10 April 2018 whilst working from Silverknowes to Gorebridge.

(Image 89): Vehicle 840/SN57 DDJ passes South St David Street on 18 July 2019 whilst working from Silverknowes to Penicuik Deanburn.

1.3.5: FLEET NUMBER 301–400; 926–936; 951–960
Volvo B9TL with Wrightbus Gemini 2 bodywork

This fleet was delivered in five batches; 301–329 between March and July 2009, 330–350 between September and December 2009, 351–400 between June and July 2011, 926–936 between April and July 2009 and 951–960 between June and July 2011. A sixth batch, 937–950, was delivered in March 2010 for Airlink services (see Section 2) and subsequently transferred to Lothian Country Buses when that company was established to take over abandoned East Lothian services. Some of the vehicles were allocated to Route 26 services that passed Edinburgh Zoo and hence received animal vinyls to promote the zoo whilst other vehicles received route identification branding identifying both Route 22 (Ocean Terminal–Gyle Centre) and Route 26 (Tranent/Seton Sands–Clerwood) services.

(Image 90): Vehicle 305/SN09 CTX displays its Harlequin design livery and the orange route identification for the Tranent–Clerwood service that it is working on 20 August 2011 when passing along Princes Street.

A pink colour was applied as route identification to Route 22 services (Ocean Terminal–Gyle Centre), including to vehicles bearing the Harlequin livery design.

(Image 91): Vehicle 331/SN59 BFM passes Jenners department store (a famous Edinburgh landmark) on 20 August 2011 whilst working from the Gyle Centre to the Ocean Terminal.

(Image 92): Vehicle 336/SN59 BFX passes Princes Street East Gardens on a wet 15 September 2014 whilst working from the Ocean Terminal to Gyle Centre.

(Image 93): Vehicle 350/SN59 BHF passes Princes Street East Gardens on a wet 15 September 2014 whilst working from the Gyle Centre to the Ocean Terminal; note the incorrect destination blind which had not been changed at the Gyle Centre terminus.

(Image 94): Vehicle 334/SN59 BFU passes the Waverley Bridge junction on 20 August 2011 whilst working from the Ocean Terminal to the Gyle Centre. Note the incorrect destination blind which had not been changed at the Ocean Terminal terminus.

(Image 95): Vehicle 935/SN09 CVW, devoid of Route Identifier, passes the Balmoral Hotel (previously the North British Hotel) on 22 August 2011 as it prepares to turn onto North Bridge whilst working from Clovenstone to Mayfield.

Vehicles allocated to Route 26 (Tranent/Seton Sands–Clerwood), which passed Edinburgh Zoo, were fitted with vinyls commemorating animals resident at the zoo as part of the promotions advertising the zoo. Examples of vehicles with such branding include …

(Image 96): … vehicle 302/SN09 CTO bearing Penguin vinyls and orange route identification branding as it passes Pinkhill on 3 June 2015 whilst working from Clerwood to Tranent.

(Image 97): … vehicle 309/SN09 CUC bearing gorilla vinyls and orange route identification branding on 11 September 2015 as it passes along Princes Street whilst working from Clerwood to Seton Sands.

(Image 98): … vehicle 323/SN09 CVD bearing zebra vinyls and orange route identification branding on 20 August 2011 as it passes along Princes Street whilst working from Clerwood to Tranent.

Right (Image 99): ... vehicle 304/SN09 CTV bearing blue poison arrow frog vinyls and orange route identification branding on 29 June 2015 as it pulls away from a bus-stop adjacent to Princes Street East Gardens whilst working from Tranent to Clerwood.

Right (Image 100): ... vehicle 320/SN09 CVA bearing tiger vinyls and orange route identification branding on 20 August 2011 as it passes along Princes Street whilst working from Seton Sands to Clerwood.

Below (Image 101): ... vehicle 307/SN09 CTZ bearing flamingo vinyls and orange route identification branding on 29 June 2015 as it pulls away from a bus-stop adjacent to Princes Street East Gardens whilst working from Tranent to Clerwood.

The route identification branding was initially retained when the Flowline design was introduced in 2013 but was gradually removed from service.

(Image 102): Vehicle 311/ SN09 CUH bears both Flowline design and orange route identification branding on 24 June 2015 as it passes Frederick Street whilst working from Clerwood to Seton Sands.

(Image 103): Vehicle 327/ SN09 CVH bears Flowline design and orange route identification branding, albeit without route number, as it passes Princes Street East Gardens on a wet 15 September 2014 whilst working from Seton Sands to Clerwood.

(Image 104): Vehicle 337/ SN09 BFY bears only the Flowline design on 12 April 2019 as it passes Frederick Street whilst working from Riccarton to Restalrig. Note also that the Transport for Edinburgh (TfE) text that normally appears above the driver's window has been replaced with the 1919 100 Years 2019 text that was applied to the Lothian Buses fleet during the centenary year of public ownership.

(Image 105): Vehicle 348/SN59 BHD bears both Flowline livery and route identification branding on 29 June 2015 as it passes along Princes Street whilst working from the Ocean Terminal to Gyle Centre.

(Image 106): Vehicle 960/ SN11 EAP, bearing the Angular livery design, turns out of Leith Street onto Waterloo Place on 5 May 2022 whilst working from The Jewel to Hillend.

(Image 107): Vehicle 933/SN09 CYU bears the Flowline livery design and tangerine route identification branding on 24 June 2015 as it turns out of Frederick Street onto Princes Street whilst working from Silverknowes to Gorebridge.

(Image 108): Vehicle 926/SN09 CVL bears the Flowline livery design and tangerine route identifier on 11 September 2015 as it calls at a Princes Street bus-stop whilst working from Silverknowes to Gilmerton.

(Image 109): Vehicle 926/SN09 CVL bears the Flowline livery design and tangerine route identifier on 24 June 2015 as it passes South St David Street whilst working from Gilmerton to Silverknowes.

(Image 110): Vehicle 960/SN11 EAP bears the Angular livery design on 21 August 2021 as it approaches Princes Street from North Bridge whilst working from Hunter's Tryst to The Jewel.

1.3.6: FLEET NUMBER 201–215
ADL Enviro 400 with Alexander – Dennis bodywork
This small batch of experimental hybrid vehicles was delivered between August and September 2011 and were initially operated on the Western Harbour–Torphin/Bonaly service. To denote their electric power source they were initially delivered in the Flowline livery design but with the white replaced by dark cream which was later applied to the Volvo 7900H fleet (see Section 1.2.5). They were later re-liveried into a revised madder/white livery design when individual vehicles were converted to diesel only operation; the fleet was subsequently sold out of service during 2022.

Left (Image 111): Vehicle 201/SN11 EES bears original livery on 24 June 2015 as it turns out of South St David Street onto Princes Street whilst working from Western Harbour to Torphin.

Below: (Image 112): Vehicle 209/SN61 BBU bears an interim revised madder/white livery design on 28 October 2017 as it passes Princes Street Gardens whilst working from Western Harbour to Bonaly.

(Image 113): Vehicle 207/SN61 BBK bears an interim revised madder/white livery design on 18 July 2019 as it turns from South St David Street onto Princes Street whilst working from Western Harbour to Torphin.

(Image 114): Vehicle 203/LB61 HYB bears the Angular design of livery with rounded edges on 18 July 2019 as it turns from South St David Street onto Princes Street whilst working from Western Harbour to Torphin.

1.3.7: FLEET NUMBER 401–425
Volvo B5TL with Wrightbus Gemini 3 bodywork
This fleet was delivered as the first of a number of batches between November and December 2014, after which the Gemini 3 bodywork was re-styled for subsequent batches 426–510 (see Section 1.3.8)

(Image 115): Vehicle 407/BN64 CPU was delivered in the Flowline livery design as noted on 11 September 2015 as it passed Princes Street Gardens whilst working from Mayfield to Clovenstone.

(Image 116): Vehicle 405/BN64 CPK bears the revised Angular livery design on 18 July 2019 as it passes South St David Street whilst working from Wester Hailes to Sheriffhall.

1.3.8: FLEET NUMBER 426–510
Volvo B5TL with re-styled Wrightbus Gemini 3 bodywork

This fleet was delivered in four batches following a re-design of the Gemini 3 bodywork (see Section 1.3.7); 426–437 were initially supplied for Airport 100 services in June 2015, 441–465 between December 2016 and January 2017, 466–495 between May and July 2017 and 496–510 being delivered to Airlink 100 services between July and August 2017. After a short period, the 426–437 batch reverted to city services and the 496 - 510 batch was transferred to the new Skylink group of services (see Section 3).

Right (Image 117): Vehicle 456/SJ66 LPX enters Princes Street from South St David Street on 18 July 2019 whilst working from Wallyford to Balerno. Note the re-styled front end and the Angular livery design which subsequently became the corporate livery design.

Below (Image 118): Vehicle 469/SF17 VND enters Princes Street from South St David Street on 12 April 2019 whilst working from Tranent to Clerwood.

(Image 119): Vehicle 441/SJ66 LOA was the first city vehicle to bear the new angular livery design as seen on 19 April 2017 when it passed the Sir Walter Scott Monument whilst working from the Ocean Terminal to the Gyle Centre.

(Image 120): Vehicle 429/ SA15 VTG was initially allocated to Airport 100 services but subsequently transferred to city services as on 12 April 2019 when it passed Princes Street Gardens whilst working from Mayfield to Clovenstone.

(Image 121): Vehicle 495/ SF17 VOJ displays its Giraffe vinyls promoting Edinburgh Zoo on 21 August 2019 as it passes the entrance to Princes Street Gardens whilst working from Tranent to Clerwood.

1.3.9: FLEET NUMBER 551–590
Volvo B5LH Hybrid with re-styled Wrightbus Gemini 3 bodywork
This fleet was delivered in two batches following a re-design of the Gemini 3 bodywork (see Section 1.3.7); 551–570 being delivered between July and August 2015 and 571–590 being delivered in September 2017. The second batch was initially allocated to the Skyline services, but some vehicles were subsequently transferred to city services and other Lothian Buses companies.

(Image 122): Vehicle 551/SA15 VUB, bearing Lothian Buses' Poppy livery, passes Princes Street East Gardens on 5 May 2022 whilst working from the Ocean Terminal to Heriot-Watt University.

(Image 123): Vehicle 553/SA15 VUD passes along Princes Street on 29 June 2016 whilst working from Clovenstone to Mayfield.

Right (Image 124): Vehicle 590/SJ67 MHF enters Waterloo Place from Leith Street on 5 May 2022 whilst working from the Ocean Terminal to Heriot-Watt University.

Below (Image 125): Vehicle 555/SA15 VUF approaches a bus-stop adjacent to Princes Street East Gardens on 21 August 2021 whilst working from the Ocean Terminal to Heriot-Watt University.

1.3.10: FLEET NUMBER 1000–1050
Volvo B9TL with Wrightbus Gemini 2 bodywork

This fleet was bought from the London Central Bus franchise of London Transport in 2017 following an upgrade of the latter's fleet. The fleet was originally delivered to London in two batches between September and October 2010 and between December 2011 and February 2012. When bought by Lothian Buses they were re-furbished by Wrightbus, re-registered and entered service with Lothian Buses during 2018. The fleet was shared between Lothian Buses city fleet and Lothian Country Buses (see Section 3.3.1.5) for services in West Lothian.

An early service using this batch of vehicles was that between Silverknowes and Gorebridge; examples of vehicles noted preparing to turn off Princes Street onto Frederick Street on this service on 12 April 2019 included …

Right (Image 126):
… vehicle 1021/LXZ 5406.

Below (Image 127):
… vehicle 1020/LXZ 5405.

(Image 128): Vehicle 1005/LXZ 5387 passes the Sir Walter Scott Monument on 21 August 2021 whilst working from Sheriffhall to Wester Hailes.

(Image 129): Vehicle 1050/LXZ 5438 approaches the South St David Street junction with Princes Street on 18 July 2019 whilst working from Silverknowes to Gorebridge.

1.3.11: FLEET NUMBER 1051–1062
Volvo B5TL with Wrightbus Gemini 3 bodywork

This small fleet order of twelve vehicles was delivered between April and May 2018 as a follow-on order to the previous order (see Section 1.3.8) delivered between June 2015 and August 2017.

Right (Image 130): Vehicle 1051/SJ18 NFA approaches Princes Street from North Bridge on 12 April 2019 whilst working from the Royal Infirmary to Muirhouse.

Below (Image 131): Vehicle 1061/SJ18 NFN passes along Princes Street on 21 August 2021 whilst working from Western Harbour to Torphin.

1.3.12: FLEET NUMBER 1063–1140
Volvo B8TL with Alexander - Dennis Enviro 400 XLB bodywork

To celebrate the century of Lothian Buses operation in 2019, Lothian Buses and Volvo designed a new tri-axle chassis with Alexander-Dennis providing the bodywork. The fleet was delivered in two batches; 1063–1104 between January and March 2019 and 1105–1125 between May and June 2019 whilst a third batch (1126–1140) was delivered for Airlink 100 services (see Section 3.1.1.4). Vehicles 1126–1130 were subsequently transferred to the city fleet but, as at September 2022, have yet to receive the corporate livery hence are operating in base white without vinyls. Some vehicles (1063/1068–1071/1083/1093/ 1104) were delivered with SG68 registrations but all except 1063 were later re-registered with SJ19 registrations.

(Image 132): Vehicle 1099/SJ19 OXS passes along Princes Street on 5 May 2022 whilst working from East Craigs to Bonnyrigg.

(Image 133): Vehicle 1063/SG68 LCA passes Princes Street East Gardens on 21 August 2021 whilst working from the Ocean Terminal to Hyvots Bank.

(Image 134): Vehicle 1087/SJ19 OXC turns out of South St David Street onto Princes Street on 18 July 2019 whilst working from Silverknowes to Colinton.

(Image 135): Vehicle 1071/SJ19 OWF enters Princes Street from Waterloo Place on 21 August 2021 whilst en route to start its day of duty on a city service.

Opposite above (Image 136): Vehicle 1125/SJ19 OZD was given a special livery to commemorate the centenary of Lothian Buses as a public operator which comprised madder and cream colours with ten roundels, each commemorating an event within a particular decade. 1125 was noted halting on Princes Street, adjacent to Princes Street Gardens, on 4 March 2020 whilst working from Bonnyrigg to East Craigs.

Opposite below (Image 137): At the end of the centennial celebrations, the commemorative livery was replaced by giraffe print vinyls to promote Edinburgh Zoo's latest acquisition of giraffes. 1125 was noted approaching a set of traffic lights on Princes Street on 5 May 2022 whilst working from East Craigs to Bonnyrigg.

A visit to the South St David Street junction with Princes Street on 18 July 2019 noted …

(Image 138): … vehicle 1095/ SJ19 OXM turning from South St David Street onto Princes Street whilst working from Silverknowes to Colinton.

(Image 139): … vehicle 1068/SJ19 OWB turning from South St David Street onto Princes Street whilst working from the Ocean Terminal to Hyvots Bank.

(Image 140): Transferred from Airlink 100 service to the city fleet, but yet to receive the city's corporate livery, vehicle 1128/SB19 GLY pulls away from a bus-stop adjacent to Princes Street East Gardens on 21 August 2021 whilst working from Bonnyrigg to East Craigs.

1.3.13: FLEET NUMBER 1141–1153
Volvo B9TL with Wrightbus Gemini 2 bodywork

Following the successful purchase of vehicles from London Transport (see Section 1.3.10) a further batch of thirteen vehicles was bought from the same operator and, after refurbishment, were introduced to Lothian Buses service during 2019.

A visit to Princes Street on 21 August 2021 noted Hillend – The Jewel services being operated by …

Right (Image 141):
… vehicle 1144/LX60 DXG as it passed along Princes Street

Below (Image 142):
… vehicle 1150/LX11 CWO as it passed along Princes Street.

1.3.14: FLEET NUMBER 291–294
BYD/Alexander - Dennis with Alexander–Dennis bodywork
This fleet of four all-electric vehicles was delivered in June 2021; sponsored by SP Energy Networks, they use batteries developed by Chinese company BYD (Build Your Dreams) in conjunction with Alexander–Dennis. The vehicles were initially trialled on the Western Harbour - Bonaly / Torphin service before being trialled on the more demanding Trinity - Greenbank service.

(Image 143): Vehicle 293/LG21 JDO turns from South St David Street onto Princes Street on 17 August 2021 whilst working from Western Harbour to Torphin.

Opposite above (Image 144): Vehicle 294/LG21 JDK passes Princes Street East Gardens on 17 August 2021 whilst working from Western Harbour to Bonaly.

Opposite below (Image 145): Vehicle 293/LG21 JDO crosses Princes Street by the Hanover Street/The Mound intersection on 5 May 2022 whilst working from Greenbank to Trinity and passes sister vehicle 291/LG21 JDF working from Trinity to Greenbank.

1.3.15: FLEET NUMBER 601–698
Volvo B5TL With Alexander–Dennis bodywork

Following concerns with the performance of the latest Wrightbus-bodied vehicles and the entering into administration of the company, the latest order placed with Volvo specified Alexander–Dennis bodywork. The order was delivered in two batches; 601–650 between May and July 2021 and 651–698 between October 2021 and February 2022.

(Image 146): Vehicle 601/SJ21 MYA passes the Hanover Street/The Mound intersection of Princes Street on 21 August 2021 whilst working from Balerno to Wallyford.

(Image 147): Vehicle 602/SJ21 MYB calls at the bus-stop adjacent to Princes Street East Gardens on 21 August 2021 whilst working from Restalrig to Heriot-Watt University.

Above left (Image 148): Vehicle 609/SJ21 MYL pulls away from a bus-stop adjacent to Princes Street East Gardens on 21 August 2021 whilst working from Restalrig to Heriot-Watt University.

Above right (Image 149): Vehicle 623/SJ21 MZF enters Princes Street from Waterloo Place on 5 May 2022 whilst working from Wallyford to Balerno.

Below (Image 150): Vehicle 643/SJ21 NBM passes South St Davids Street on a dreich 21 August 2021 whilst working from King's Road to Granton.

SECTION 2: EDINBURGH BUS TOURS

An integral part of the Lothian Buses operations is the tour programme which, as at September 2022, operates 6 tour programmes covering routes within the city including one to the Forth Bridges that incorporates a Forth cruise.

At the beginning of the era in 2011 there were three main tours which began from Waverley Bridge and were operated by a fleet of redundant Dennis Trident SLF double deck vehicles (501–530) which had been converted between 2007–12 to open-top bodies and dedicated to the three tours. These were the City Sightseeing tour using vehicles 501–510 rebuilt between 2007–08, Edinburgh Tour tour using vehicles 511–520 rebuilt between March and June 2010 and Majestic Tours tour using vehicles 521–528 rebuilt between August 2010 and February 2011. Vehicles 529 and 530 were rebuilt during August 2012 for Edinburgh Tours and used as standby vehicles for the tour programme.

In September 2016, the fleet was replaced by a delivery of brand new Volvo B5TL buses with Wrightbus Gemini 3 open-top bodies; vehicles 221–230 were branded for City Sightseeing tours, 231–241 were branded for Edinburgh Tour tours, 242–248 were branded for Majestic Tours tours and 249–250 were branded for Edinburgh Tours to act as standby vehicles.

In 2007, a fourth tour covering the Forth Bridges was initiated by Lothian Buses, initially also using redundant Dennis Trident SLF vehicles but subsequent renewals used redundant Volvo vehicles from the city fleet to operate this service.

The fifth tour programme is that of MAC Tours which began operating as a private company in 1998 using converted ex-London Transport RouteMaster buses to initiate a tour programme of Edinburgh. The company was taken over by Lothian Buses in April 2002 whilst retaining both its vehicles and branding.

All these tour programmes were operated from Waverley Bridge but in June 2020 a road improvement scheme for the bridge resulted in the start point transferring to St Andrews Square.

In 2022, Lothian Buses initiated a sixth tour named Cobbles Tour for which it transferred vehicles 230–234 from the City Sightseeing fleet and re-liveried them for the new tour.

2.1: CITY SIGHTSEEING TOUR
Starting at Waverley Bridge (St Andrews Square since June 2020) this tour visits the Old Town, New Town, Calton Hill, Holyrood Palace and Edinburgh Castle.

2.1.1: FLEET NUMBER 501–510; 531–533;
Dennis Trident SLF with Alexander bodywork
This fleet was transferred from the city fleet after conversion between 2007–08 (see Section 1.3.1)

(Image 151): Vehicle 502/T502 SSG approaches the Palace of Holyrood on 11 September 2015 during its tour circuit.

A visit to Edinburgh on 29 June 2015 noted this tour passing Princes Street East Gardens being operated by …

(Image 152): … vehicle 503/T503 SSG.

(Image 153): … vehicle 508/ T508 SSG.

2.1.2: FLEET NUMBER 221 - 230
Volvo B5TL with Wrightbus Gemini 3 Open - Top bodywork
This fleet was introduced to service in September 2016 with dedicated vinyls.

(Image 154): Vehicle 224/SJ16 CSV passes Princes Street Gardens on 5 May 2022 during its tour circuit.

(Image 155): Vehicle 223/SJ16 CSU collects passengers at the Waverley Bridge tour start point on 10 April 2018.

(Image 156): Vehicle 223/SJ16 CSU pulls away from the tour start point on 19 April 2017 as it begins its tour circuit.

2.2: EDINBURGH TOUR

Starting at Waverley Bridge (St Andrews Square since June 2020) this tour visits the Old Town, New Town, Calton Hill, Holyrood Palace and Edinburgh Castle but follows a different route from the City Sightseeing tour (see Section 2.1)

2.2.1: FLEET NUMBER 511–520

Dennis Trident SLF with Plaxton President bodywork

This fleet was transferred from the city fleet after conversion between March and June 2010 (see Section 1.3.1)

Above (Image 157): Vehicle 510/T510 SSG, transferred from the City Sightseeing fleet (see Section 2.1.1), pulls away from the Waverley Bridge start point on 5 August 2015 as it begins the tour circuit.

Left (Image 158): Vehicle 511/T511 SSG approaches Princes Street on 22 August 2011 as it begins its tour circuit.

(Image 159): Vehicle 509/T509 SSG, transferred from the City Sightseeing fleet, arrives at the Waverley Bridge start point on 18 December 2015 in preparation for another tour circuit.

2.2.2: FLEET NUMBER 231–241
Volvo B5TL with Wrightbus Gemini 3 Open–Top bodywork
This fleet was introduced to service in September 2016 with dedicated vinyls.

(Image 160): Vehicle 237/SJ16 ZZA stands on Waverley Bridge on 4 March 2020 awaiting the start of its next tour circuit. Note the liveries of the City Sightseeing and Majestic tours on the vehicles parked behind 237.

(Image 161): Vehicle 236/SJ16 CTZ traverses the Hanover Street/The Mound intersection of Princes Street on 10 April 2018 whilst working a tour circuit.

(Image 162): Vehicle 241/SJ16 ZZE turns into Frederick Street on 5 May 2022 whilst working an Edinburgh Tours tour circuit.

2.3: MAJESTIC TOUR

Starting at Waverley Bridge (St Andrews Square since June 2020) this tour makes a long loop of the city that includes Holyrood Palace and the New Town via the Royal Botanic Gardens and the Ocean Terminal - the home of the de-commissioned Royal Yacht 'Britannia'.

2.3.1: FLEET NUMBER 521–528

Dennis Trident SLF with Plaxton President bodywork

This fleet was transferred from the city fleet after conversion between August 2010 and February 2011 (see Section 1.3.1).

(Image 163): Vehicle 524/V524 ESC pulls away from the tour start point on 22 August 2011 whilst en route to Annandale Street garage at the end of its tour of duty.

(Image 164): Vehicle 526/V526 ESC stands on Waverley Bridge on 22 August 2011 awaiting the start of its next tour circuit.

(Image 165): Vehicle 523/V523 ESC stands at Ocean Terminal on 30 June 2015 whilst working a tour circuit.

(Image 166): Vehicle 523/V523 ESC turns from Princes Street onto South St David Street on 5 August 2015 whilst working a tour circuit.

2.3.2: FLEET NUMBER 242–248
Volvo B5TL with Wrightbus Gemini 3 Open–Top bodywork
This fleet was introduced to service in September 2016 with dedicated vinyls.

(Image 167): Vehicle 245/SJ16 ZZK prepares to turn from Princes Street onto Frederick Street on 12 April 2019 whilst working a tour circuit.

(Image 168): Vehicle 247/SJ16 ZZO awaits departure from Waverley Bridge on 28 October 2017 whilst working a tour circuit.

The tour circuit nears its end by crossing Princes Street over the Hanover Street / The Mound intersection as noted on …

(Image 169): … 28 October 2017 by vehicle 244/SJ16 ZZH.

(Image 170): … on 5 May 2022 by vehicle 248/SJ16 ZZP.

2.4: SPARE VEHICLES
This pair of vehicles are standby vehicles operated on any of the tour circuits as and when required

2.4.1: FLEET NUMBER 249 AND 250
Volvo B5TL with Wrightbus Gemini 3 Open–Top bodywork
This fleet was introduced to service between October and November 2016 with dedicated vinyls.

Left (Image 171):
Vehicle 249/ SJ66 LKO stands on Waverley Bridge on 10 April 2018 whilst in use as a Driver Route Learning vehicle.

Below (Image 172):
Vehicle 250/SJ66 LKP enters Princes Street from Waterloo Place on 21 August 2021 whilst in use as a Driver Route Learning vehicle.

2.5: COBBLES TOUR
This tour was first introduced for the 2022 season and saw five vehicles transferred from the Edinburgh Tour fleet. The new tour started from Lawnmarket and made a circuit of the inner city including Greyfriars Kirk, Holyrood Palace and Charlotte Square.

2.5.1: FLEET NUMBER 230–234
Volvo B5TL with Wrightbus Gemini 3 Open–Top bodywork
This fleet was transferred from the Edinburgh Tours vehicle fleet (see Section 2.2.2).

(Image 173): Vehicle 230/SJ16 CTK passes the South St Andrews Street junction with Princes Street on 5 May 2022 whilst working a tour circuit.

(Image 174): Vehicle 233/SJ16 CTV crosses Princes Street by the Hanover Street/The Mound intersection on 5 May 2022 whilst working a tour circuit.

2.6: MAC TOURS

MAC Tours was a private company initiated in 1998 using ex-London Transport RouteMaster buses but it was bought by Lothian Buses in 2002 to become part of the Edinburgh Tours operation whilst retaining both its original livery and branding. The tour operates over a circuit encompassing the New Town, Edinburgh Castle, Holyrood Palace and the Old Town.

2.6.1: FLEET NUMBER 289–300
AEC Chassis with Park Royal bodywork
This fleet was purchased from London Transport and included vehicles built in 1960 (with prefix registration VLT) and 1965 (registration CUV [n] C).

Above left (Image 175): RouteMaster VLT 281 (delivered to London Transport as fleet number RM281 in 1960)/Lothian Buses fleet number 300 passes Princes Street East Gardens on 15 September 2014 whilst working a tour circuit.

Above right (Image 176): RouteMaster CUV 248C (delivered to London Transport as fleet number RCL 2248 in 1965)/Lothian Buses fleet number 290 turns onto Princes Street from Lothian Road on 29 June 2015 whilst working a tour circuit.

Left (Image 177): RouteMaster CUV 241C (delivered to London Transport as fleet number RCL 2241 in 1965)/Lothian Buses fleet number 289 crosses Waverley Bridge on 29 June 2016 whilst working a tour circuit.

2.7: 3 BRIDGES TOURS

This tour was introduced for the 2007 season and encompassed a journey from Waverley Bridge (St Andrews Square since June 2020) to South Queensferry where a transfer is made to a ferry boat tour of the Firth of Forth from Hawes Pier. The ferry operates along the Fife coastline to Blackness Castle then returns to South Queensferry following the West Lothian coastline thence returns by bus to Edinburgh. A feature of this tour is the identification of scenes from Robert Louis Stevenson's famous novel *Kidnapped*, including the Hawes Inn opposite the pier, which features strongly in the book.

2.7.1: FLEET NUMBER 650–651
Dennis Trident SLF with Plaxton President bodywork

This fleet was transferred from the city fleet after conversion and re-registration (see Section 1.3.1).

(Image 178): Vehicle 651/XIL 1484, originally registered to the city fleet as SK52 OHN, carries early tour livery on 5 August 2015 as it turns from Princes Street onto South St David Street at the start of its tour circuit.

(Image 179): Vehicle 650/XIL 1483, originally registered to the city fleet as SK52 OHL, bears the later tour livery on 10 April 2018 as it passes Princes Street East Gardens at the start of its tour circuit.

2.7.2: FLEET NUMBER 905–906
Volvo B9TL with Wrightbus Gemini 1 bodywork
This fleet was transferred from the city fleet after conversion and re-livery (see Section 1.3.4).

(Image 180): Vehicle 905/SN08 BXV passes Princes Street Gardens on 12 April 2019 whilst nearing the end of its tour circuit at Waverley Bridge. Compare the livery with that applied when operating with the city fleet (see Image 83).

(Image 181): Vehicle 906/SN08 BXW approaches the end of its tour circuit as it passes along Princes Street on 5 May 2022.

SECTION 3: COUNTRY SERVICES

In parallel with the changes within the city boundary between 2011 and 2022, Lothian Buses has also undertaken developments with the transport services of neighbouring East and West Lothian by extending the range of services which serve the capital's hinterland. In 1923, ECT had signed agreements with Scottish Motor Traction (SMT), later to become Eastern Scottish, that effectively co-ordinated the services of both companies whereby ECT would undertake transport within the city boundary and SMT would undertake transport outside the city boundary with special fare conditions for passengers travelling only within the city boundary. Following the de-regulation of bus services in 1975, the SMT services were undertaken by both First Group and Stagecoach as they obtained the rights to operate the many individual services.

This re-structuring initially led to the creation of Lothian Region Transport to operate both services within the city boundary and some of the services to areas once operated by SMT that had now been brought within the expanding city limits as part of the boundary changes imposed in the 1970s. The growth of the city, accompanied by the development of a new tramway system connecting the city to the airport, led to the creation Transport for Edinburgh (TfE) in 2013 to oversee the integration of transport within the Lothian region with Lothian Buses represented on the body.

Whilst Lothian Buses operates the city services and, in support of tourism, operates Airlink and Skylink services between the airport and the city and a mix of tourist services within the city, the company has also created new companies to replace the services abandoned by both First Group and Stagecoach as they withdrew from the service provision on the grounds of cost. Lothian Buses has created Lothian Country Buses and East Coast Buses as separate companies within the Lothian Buses family to provide these services, initially by supplying buses from within the city fleet to the nascent companies as they began the takeover of service provision.

As with Section 1, this section reflects the services as they operate in and around Princes Street as the centre of Edinburgh thereby showing the commonality of Lothian Buses in the liveries and fleets of the Lothian Buses family, whilst still retaining the appeal of the local identity within their individual spheres of operation.

3.1 LINK SERVICES

In parallel with the city services, Lothian Buses operates a 24-hour service of express buses between the city centre at Waverley Bridge (St Andrews Square since June 1920) and the airport designated Airlink. The main service is Route 100 from Waverley Bridge, adjacent to Waverley Station, but in June 2020 the road was closed for improvements to be made, hence a new terminal point was created at St Andrews Square and a new start point was created at South St David Street. The Airlink service is supported by a further three services operating under the Skylink banner which serve other parts of the city and all are operated with a dedicated fleet of vehicles which are usually retained for about three years before being replaced and transferred to other Lothian Buses company operations.

3.1.1: AIRPORT 100

3.1.1.1: FLEET NUMBER 937–950
Volvo B9TL with Wrightbus Gemini 2 bodywork
This fleet was delivered as the sixth batch of this series of vehicles (see Section 1.3.5); 937–950 were delivered in March 2010 for Airlink services and subsequently transferred to Lothian Country Buses when that company was initially established to provide East Lothian services. (see Section 3.2.1.4)

(Image 182): Vehicle 950/LB10 BUS traverses Princes Street on a dreich 15 September 2014 whilst working a Waverley Bridge–Airport service.

(Image 183): Vehicle 940/SN10 DKK enters Princes Street from Shandwick Place on 29 June 2015 whilst working from the Airport to Waverley Bridge.

(Image 184): Vehicle 947/SN10 DLD passes Pinkhill on 3 June 2015 whilst working from Waverley Bridge to the Airport.

(Image 185): Dusk falls as vehicle 950/ LB10 BUS passes Princes Street East Gardens on 2 June 2015 whilst working from Waverley Bridge to the Airport.

3.1.1.2: FLEET NUMBER 426–437
Volvo B5TL with re-styled Wrightbus Gemini 3 bodywork
This fleet was delivered as the first of four batches (see Section 1.3.8) that received the re-styled bodywork when delivered in June 2015. This batch only operated for a short time in Airlink service and was quickly transferred to the city fleet when replaced by a later batch of vehicles in August 2017 (see Section 1.3.8).

(Image 186): Vehicle 427/SA15 VTE heads a pair of vehicles with re-designed Gemini 3 bodywork as they park on Waverley Bridge on 5 August 2015 whilst awaiting their next service to the airport.

(Image 187): Vehicle 437/SA15 VTT parks on Waverley Bridge on 22 July 2016 whilst providing an evening service to the airport as part of the 24-hour daily timetable.

(Image 188): Vehicle 433/SA15 VTM stands on Waverley Bridge on 11 September 2015 whilst awaiting customers departing to the airport.

(Image 189): Vehicle 430/SA15 VTJ passes Princes Street East Gardens on 11 September 2015 whilst working from Waverley Bridge to the airport.

3.1.1.3: FLEET NUMBER 496–510
Volvo B5TL with re-styled Wrightbus Gemini 3 bodywork
This fleet was delivered as the fourth of four batches (see Section 1.3.8) that received the re-styled bodywork; delivered between July and August 2017, this batch replaced the earlier batch 426–437 (see Section 3.1.1.2). This fleet bore the Angular livery design, adopted as the corporate livery from 2016 with madder and white colours being replaced by blue and light grey.

(Image 190): Vehicle 500/SF17 VOU heads a line of three vehicles parked on Waverley Bridge on 10 April 2018 awaiting their next service to the airport.

(Image 191): Vehicle 498/SF17 VOO stands after its arrival at Waverley Bridge on 18 July 2019 whilst working from the airport to Waverley Bridge.

(Image 192): Vehicle 506/SF17 VPE passes Princes Street Gardens on 12 April 2019 whilst working a Waverley Bridge–Airport service.

(Image 193): Vehicle 509/SF17 VPK crosses Princes Street by the Hanover Street/The Mound intersection on 10 April 2018 whilst positioning for an arrival on Waverley Bridge with a service from the airport.

3.1.1.4: FLEET NUMBER 1126–1140
Volvo B8TL with Alexander–Dennis Enviro 400 XLB bodywork

This fleet was delivered as the third of three batches (see Section 1.3.12) delivered between July and August 2019 and replaced the earlier batch 496–510 (see Section 3.1.1.3). Vehicles 1126–1130 were subsequently transferred to the city fleet without vinyls and, as at September 2022, are still awaiting re-liverying from base white to the corporate madder and white colour scheme.

(Image 194): Vehicle 1126/SB19 GLK stands on Waverley Bridge on 4 March 2020 as passengers board its Waverley Bridge–Airport service.

(Image 195): Vehicle 1136/SB19 GMY pulls away from its revised South St Davids Street start point on 21 August 2021 and turns onto Princes Street whilst working a service to the airport.

One of the few stops within the city limits is at Haymarket Interchange where, on 4 March 2020, the Waverley Bridge – Airport service was provided by …

(Image 196): … vehicle 1128/SB19 GLY. This vehicle was subsequently transferred to the city fleet where, as at September 2022, it awaits its city corporate livery.

(Image 197): … vehicle 1132/SB19 GMO.

3.1.2: SKYLINK

In late 2017, Lothian Buses created three further services to Edinburgh Airport that operated under the Skylink branding and used vehicles from the Volvo B5LH/Wrightbus Gemini 3 deliveries (fleet numbers 571–590). To identify them as dedicated vehicles they adopted the city design of livery but replaced the madder portion by blue and carried 'Skylink' branding.

The three routes forming the Skylink group of services were:

(i) Skylink 200 serving north Edinburgh and terminating at Ocean Terminal.
(ii) Skylink 300 serving west Edinburgh and terminating at Bread Street; its original terminus was Ocean Terminal.
(iii) Skylink 400 serving south Edinburgh and terminating at Fort Kinnaird.

3.1.2.1: FLEET NUMBER 426–437
Volvo B5TL with re-styled Wrightbus Gemini 3 bodywork

This fleet was initially allocated to Airlink services (see Section 3.1.1.1) but when replaced by a later batch of vehicles (fleet numbers 496 - 510) the vehicles were initially transferred to Skylink services pending final transfer to the city fleet.

(Image 198): Vehicle 431/SA15 VTK approaches Gyle Centre on 28 May 2018 whilst working from the Airport to the Ocean Terminal which was subsequently cut back to Bread Street thus serving Edinburgh's west end area. Prior to the introduction of the Skylink group of services, this service had operated as Route 35 of the city services (see Section 1.3.3).

3.1.2.2: FLEET NUMBER 571–590
Volvo B5LH with Wrightbus Gemini 3 bodywork
This group comprised vehicles transferred from the city fleet (see Section 1.2.9).

(Image 199): Vehicle 572/SJ67 MFF departs from the Gyle Centre on 28 May 2018 whilst working from the Airport to the Ocean Terminal.

(Image 200): Vehicle 571/SJ67 MFE passes the defunct Caledonian Railway Leith North terminal station as it approaches the Ocean Terminal on 28 October 2017 whilst working from the airport to the Ocean Terminal.

3.1.3: CRUISELINK SERVICES

In 2019, Lothian Buses introduced a new service to cater for the arrival of cruise ships in the Firth of Forth at South Queensferry. Cruise passengers are shipped to Hawes Pier from where a fleet of buses operate a direct service to St Andrews Square with a dedicated return service to Hawes Pier during the period of the cruise ships' anchorage. The Cruiselink has no dedicated buses but simply hires vehicles in from Lothian Buses city fleet as and when the service is operated.

On 9 September 2022 a visit by the cruise ship *Amsterdam* led to the operation of the Cruiselink service.

Left (Image 201): Vehicle 650/SJ21 NCD drops into South Queensferry whilst working a return St Andrews Square–Hawes Pier service.

Below (Image 202): Vehicle 611/SJ21 MYN stands at Hawes Pier after cruise passengers had disembarked for a return to the cruise ship and awaits its return to St Andrews Square to collect a further tranche of passengers.

Vehicles returning to Hawes Pier from St Andrews Square turn at the end of the car park to stop by the RNLI Lifeboat station as noted with the return of **(Image 203 above)** vehicle 649/SJ21 NCC and **(Image 204 below)** vehicle 678/SJ71 HKT.

SECTION 3.2: EAST LOTHIAN SERVICES

In June 2012, First Scotland East withdrew its 113 Pencaitland–Edinburgh service and Lothian Buses transferred five of its Volvo B7RLE single deck vehicles with Wrightbus Eclipse 2 bodywork (fleet numbers 195–199) to operate this service under East Lothian Buses branding. In September 2014, the withdrawal of First Scotland East's 104 Haddington–Edinburgh service saw a pair of Dennis Trident SLF double deck vehicles with Plaxton President bodywork (fleet numbers 635 and 636) transfer from the city fleet to the new company which then began operating as Lothian Country Buses. The company retained the Lothian Buses style of corporate livery but replaced the madder and white colours with green and cream reminiscent of the Scottish Motor Traction / Eastern Scottish livery, the company which had operated the services prior to de-regulation. During 2015, the Lothian Country Buses fleet was supplemented by a further transfer of Volvo B7RLE single deck vehicles plus batches of Volvo B9TL vehicles, including the fourteen Volvo B9TL vehicles (fleet numbers 937–950) displaced from the Airlink services.

In 2016, First Group East withdrew both its Musselburgh and North Berwick services, hence East Coast Buses was created by Lothian Buses to take over the services, including the express services to Edinburgh. The new company retained the corporate design of livery but replaced madder and white and green and cream with green and grey colours. In April 2017, East Coast Buses absorbed the Lothian Country Buses services and fleet hence the latter company's name was suspended.

3.2.1: LOTHIAN COUNTRY BUSES – EAST LOTHIAN

3.2.1.1: FLEET NUMBER 167–190; 193–199
Volvo B7RLE with Wrightbus Eclipse 2 bodywork
This group comprised vehicles transferred from the city fleet (see Section 1.2.3).

(Image 205): Vehicle 196/SN62 BPV passes the Sir Walter Scott Monument on 5 August 2015 whilst working from Pencaitland to the Western General Hospital.

(image 206): Vehicle 172/SN60 EOE calls at a Princes Street bus-stop on 24 June 2015 whilst working from Edinburgh West End to Haddington.

(Image 207): Vehicle 195/SN62 BNY passes Princes Street East Gardens on 29 June 2015 whilst working from Haddington to Edinburgh West End.

(Image 208): Vehicle 198/SN62 BUF passes the Frederick Street junction with Princes Street on 5 August 2015 whilst working from the Western General Hospital to Pencaitland.

3.2.1.2: FLEET NUMBER 635 AND 636
Dennis/Transbus Trident SLF with Plaxton bodywork
This group comprised vehicles transferred from the city fleet (see Section 1.3.1).

Above left (Image 209): Vehicle 635/SK52 OGT calls at a Princes Street bus-stop on 24 June 2015 whilst working from the Western General Hospital to Pencaitland. Note a sister vehicle behind 635 bearing the city's Flowline design of livery.

Above right (Image 210): Vehicle 636/SK52 OGU passes the Old Waverley Hotel on 11 September 2015 whilst working from the Western General Hospital to Pencaitland.

Left (Image 211): Vehicle 636/SK52 OGU passes the Christmas Market festivities in Princes Street East Gardens on 18 December 2015 whilst working from the Western General Hospital to Pencaitland.

3.2.1.3: FLEET NUMBER 841–850
Volvo B9TL with Wrightbus Gemini 1 bodywork
This batch of ten vehicles was refurbished and re-registered when transferred from the city fleet to Lothian Country Buses (see Section 1.3.4). When Lothian Country Buses was absorbed by East Coast Buses in April 2017, some of this batch initially received Lothian Motorcoaches grey livery rather than the light green and silver grey livery of East Coast Buses. In 2022, the vehicles gained the latest design of Angular livery with dark green/white replacing the grey livery.

Right (Image 212): Vehicle 842/MXZ 1752 retains its Lothian Country Buses branding and livery on 21 August 2021 whilst working an East Coast Buses Pencaitland–West Granton service.

Below (Image 213): Vehicle 846/MXZ 1756 bears Lothian Motorcoaches livery on 5 May 2022 whilst working an East Coast Buses Edinburgh West End–Haddington service.

3.2.1.4: FLEET NUMBER 937–950
Volvo B9TL with Wrightbus Gemini 2 bodywork

This group comprised vehicles transferred from the city's Airlink fleet (see Section 3.1.1.1). In 2022, East Coast Buses began applying the new dark green/white Angular design of livery with affected vehicles losing the 20nnn prefix of its fleet number (see Section 3.2.2.5).

Left (Image 214): Vehicle 942/SN10 DKO passes the South St David Street junction with Princes Street on 29 June 2016 whilst working from Haddington to Edinburgh West End.

Below (Image 215): Vehicle 938/SN10 DKF approaches the traffic light at the Hanover Street/The Mound intersection of Princes Street on 29 June 2015 whilst working from Pencaitland to the Western General Hospital.

3.2.2: EAST COAST BUSES

When East Coast Buses was created, it re-numbered its fleet of vehicles by adding 10000 to the single deck vehicle fleet numbers and 20000 to the double deck vehicle fleet numbers.

3.2.2.1: FLEET NUMBER 167–190; 193–199
Volvo B7RLE with Wrightbus Eclipse 2 bodywork
This group comprised vehicles transferred from the city fleet (see Section 1.2.3).

This fleet was operated on services from East Lothian as noted on 19 April 2017 when …

(Image 216): … vehicle 10196/SN62 BPV (previously city fleet number 196) accelerated past Frederick Street whilst working an Edinburgh West End–Haddington express service.

(Image 217): … vehicle 10197/SN62 BTF (previously city fleet number 197) passed Princes Street East Gardens whilst working an Edinburgh West End–North Berwick service.

3.2.2.2: FLEET NUMBER 10051–10065
Volvo B8RLE with Wrightbus Eclipse 3 bodywork
This batch of vehicles were delivered new in April 2017.

(Image 218): Vehicle 10054/SF17 VMA accelerates past Frederick Street on 18 July 2019 whilst working a Dunbar–Edinburgh West End express service.

(Image 219): Vehicle 10063/SF17 VMM enters Princes Street from Waterloo Place on 10 April 2018 whilst working a North Berwick–Edinburgh West End service.

(Image 220): Vehicle 10054/SF17 VMA passes the Hanover Street/The Mound intersection of Princes Street on 10 April 2018 whilst working a North Berwick–Edinburgh West End service.

(Image 221): Vehicle 52/SF17 VLY bears a revised fleet number (i.e. devoid of 10000) and dark green/white colours as it passes Princes Street Gardens on 5 May 2022 whilst working a Dunbar–Edinburgh West End express service.

3.2.2.3: FLEET NUMBER 20001–20008
Volvo B5TL with Wrightbus Gemini 3 bodywork
This batch of vehicles were delivered new between August 2018 and September 2018.

(Image 222): Vehicle 20001/SJ18 NFP approaches a bus-stop adjacent to Princes Street East Gardens on 21 August 2021 whilst working from North Berwick to Edinburgh West End.

(Image 223): Vehicle 20003/SJ18 NFT passes South St David Street junction with Princes Street on 18 July 2019 whilst working from Edinburgh West End to North Berwick.

(Image 224): Vehicle 20007/SG68 LBU passes South St David Street junction on 5 May 2022 whilst working from Edinburgh West End to North Berwick service. Note that immediately behind is Lothian Buses city vehicle 463/SJ66 LRN working a Gyle Centre–Ocean Terminal service that was built to the same specification and livery design with the green/grey colours replaced by madder/white colours.

(Image 225): Vehicle 20005/SJ18 NFV enters Princes Street from Waterloo Place on 21 August 2021 whilst working from North Berwick to Edinburgh West End.

Right (Image 226): Vehicle 20006/SJ18 NFX passes Princes Street East Gardens on 21 August 2021 whilst working from Haddington to Edinburgh West End.

Below (Image 227): Vehicle 20003/SJ18 NFT enters Princes Street from Waterloo Place on 12 April 2019 whilst working from North Berwick to Edinburgh West End.

3.2.2.4: FLEET NUMBER (20) 701–(20) 825
Volvo B7TL with Wrightbus Gemini 1 bodywork
This group comprised vehicles transferred from the city fleet (see Section 1.3.2).

(Image 228): Vehicle 20798/SN56 AEY (previously city fleet number 798) passes Frederick Street on 31 July 2018 whilst working from West Granton to Pencaitland.

(Image 229): Vehicle 20800/SN56 AFA (previously city fleet number 800) passes South St David Street on 31 July 2018 whilst working from West Granton to Pencaitland.

(Image 230): Vehicle 20797/SN56 AEX (previously city fleet 797) enters Princes Street from Waterloo Place on 10 April 2018 whilst working a Dunbar–Edinburgh express service.

(Image 231): Vehicle 20800/SN56 AFA (previously city fleet number 800) traverses Princes Street on 28 October 2017 whilst working from Pencaitland to West Granton.

3.2.2.5: FLEET NUMBER (20)937–(20)950
Volvo B9TL with Wrightbus Gemini 2 bodywork

This group comprised vehicles transferred when Lothian Country Buses was taken over by East Coast Buses in April 2017 (see Section 3.2.1.4).

    The initial signs of the takeover were the renumbering of the Lothian Country Buses fleet to the East Coast Buses numbering by the addition of 20000 to the fleet number but retaining Lothian Country Buses livery and branding as noted on 19 April 2017 when …

Right (Image 232):
… vehicle 20940/SN10 DKK passed the Sir Walter Scott Monument whilst working from Pencaitland to the Western General Hospital.

Below (Image 233):
… vehicle 20944/SN10 DKV called at a Princes Street bus-stop whilst working from the Western General Hospital to Pencaitland.

The ex-Lothian Country Buses fleet quickly gained the East Coast Buses light green/ light grey livery whilst still operating their original Haddington and Pencaitland services. In 2022, this batch of vehicles were re-liveried with the new Angular design of livery with dark green/white colours.

(Image 234): Vehicle 20949/SN10 DLF passes Princes Street East Gardens on 21 August 2021 whilst working from Pencaitland to West Granton.

(Image 235): Vehicle 20944/SN10 DKV enters Princes Street from Waterloo Place on 12 April 2019 whilst working from Haddington to Edinburgh West End.

(Image 236): In 2022, East Coast Buses revised its fleet numbering system and its livery. Initially the fleet lost its 10xxx/20xxx prefix as noted when vehicle 942 (previously fleet number 20942)/SN10 DKO passed Princes Street Gardens on 5 May 2022 whilst working from Pencaitland to West Granton.

(Image 237): A further change was the light green/light grey colours being changed to dark green/white as noted when vehicle 947 (previously fleet number 20947)/SN10 DLD passed the Hanover Street/The Mound intersection of Princes Street on 5 May 2022 whilst working from Haddington to Edinburgh West End.

(Image 238): Vehicle 20949/SN10 DLF passes Princes East Gardens on 4 March 2020 whilst working from Pencaitland to Crewe Toll.

SECTION 3.3: WEST LOTHIAN SERVICES

In June 2017, Stagecoach Scotland East withdrew its South Queensferry–Edinburgh service and Lothian Buses resuscitated its Lothian Country Buses company to take over the service. Operating as Routes 43/X43, Lothian Buses transferred nine Volvo B9TL vehicles with Wrightbus Gemini 2 bodywork (fleet numbers 928 - 936) and re-painted them into Lothian Country Buses green and cream livery. In 2019, First West Lothian, a subsidiary company of First Scotland East withdrew its Livingston operation resulting in Lothian Buses expanding its Lothian Country Buses operation by transferring eight Volvo B5LH vehicles with Wrightbus Gemini 3 bodywork (fleet numbers 571–578) and allocated twenty-four of the Volvo B9TL vehicles with Wrightbus Gemini 2 bodywork, which were bought from London Transport, to provide the replacement services.

3.3.1: LOTHIAN COUNTRY BUSES – WEST LOTHIAN

3.3.1.1: FLEET NUMBER 101–166
Volvo B7RLE with Wrightbus Eclipse 1 bodywork
This group comprised vehicles transferred from the city fleet (see Section 1.2.2).

(Image 239): Vehicle 107/RIG 6497, originally registered as city fleet SN04 NGX, passes along Princes Street on 4 March 2020 whilst working a Whitburn–Edinburgh Regent Road express service.

(Image 240): Vehicle 116/ SN04 NHG approaches Haymarket Interchange on 4 March 2020 whilst working a Linlithgow–Edinburgh Regent Road express service.

3.3.1.2: FLEET NUMBER 176–185
Volvo B7RLE with Wrightbus Eclipse 2 bodywork
This group comprised vehicles transferred from the city fleet (see Section 1.2.3).

Express services from West Lothian terminated at Regent Road, at the start of the A1 trunk route to London. A brief interlude at Haymarket Interchange on 4 March 2020 noted …

Left (Image 241):
… vehicle 182/ SN13 BFE pulling away whilst working an Edinburgh Regent Road–Linlithgow express service.

Below (Image 242):
… vehicle 185/ SN13 BFK pulling away whilst working an Edinburgh Regent Road–Livingston express service.

3.3.1.3: FLEET NUMBER 928–936
Volvo B9TL with Wrightbus Gemini 2 bodywork
This fleet was transferred from the city fleet (see Section 1.3.5) to provide West Lothian services, initially between Edinburgh and South Queensferry.

(Image 243): Vehicle 928/SN09 CVO passes Princes Street Gardens on 10 April 2018 whilst working from St Andrews Square to South Queensferry.

(Image 244): Vehicle 929/SN09 CVP curves out of South Queensferry Tesco on 28 May 2018 whilst working from St Andrews Square to South Queensferry.

(Image 245): Vehicle 932/SN09 CVT calls at the South Queensferry Police Station on 24 May 2018 whilst working a St Andrews Square–South Queensferry express service.

(Image 246): Vehicle 935/SN09 CVW turns from Princes Street onto Frederick Street on 12 April 2019 whilst en route to St Andrews Square with its South Queensferry–St Andrews Square service.

In 2021, the Edinburgh terminal point was changed to Regent Road in line with other Lothian Country Buses services from West Lothian.

3.3.1.4: FLEET NUMBER 571–578
Volvo B5LH with Wrightbus Gemini 3 bodywork
This fleet was transferred from the city's Skylink fleet (see Section 3.1.2.2) to provide West Lothian services. This batch of vehicles had originally been delivered to the city fleet (see Section 1.3.9) before transfer to the Skylink service.

(Image 247): Vehicle 572/SJ67 MFF calls at a Princes Street bus-stop on 12 April 2019 whilst working a Bathgate–Edinburgh Regent Road express service.

(Image 248): Vehicle 575/SJ67 MFO passes Princes Street East Gardens on 21 August 2021 whilst working a Whitburn–Edinburgh Regent Road express service.

(Image 249): Vehicle 572/SJ67 MFF passes Princes Street East Gardens on 21 August 2021 whilst working an Edinburgh Regent Road–Whitburn express service.

(Image 250): Vehicle 573/SJ67 MFK displays the new order on the Edinburgh–South Queensferry service as it passes the South Queensferry Premier Inn on 10 September 2022 whilst working from South Queensferry to Edinburgh Regent Road. The service had been truncated at George Street due to revised bus operations following the death of Queen Elizabeth II and local arrangements made for the transfer of her coffin to Holyrood Palace. The use of the Volvo B5LH fleet had resulted from the withdrawal of the previous B9TL vehicles from service during 2022.

Above left (Image 251): Vehicle 572/SJ67 MFF pulls away from a bus-stop adjacent to Princes Street Gardens on 5 May 2022 whilst working from Edinburgh Regent Road to Whitburn.

Above right (Image 252): Vehicle 576/SJ67 MFP passes the South St David Street junction with Princes Street on 18 July 2019 whilst working from Whitburn to Edinburgh Regent Road.

(Image 253): Vehicle 593/LP11 YBA traverses Princes Street on 12 April 2019 whilst working from Edinburgh Regent Road to Bathgate. This vehicle was one of four Volvo B5LH buses with Wrightbus Gemini 2 bodywork that were originally sold to Bullock's of Cheadle but bought by Lothian Buses, refurbished and entered service in 2018 with Lothian Country Buses for West Lothian services.

3.3.1.5: FLEET NUMBER 1000–1050
Volvo B9TL with Wrightbus Gemini 2 bodywork

This fleet was bought from the London Central Bus franchise of London Transport in 2017 following an upgrade of the latter's fleet. The fleet was originally delivered to London in two batches between September and October 2010 and between December 2011 and February 2012. When bought by Lothian Buses, they were refurbished by Wrightbus, re-registered and entered service with Lothian Buses during 2018. The fleet was shared between Lothian Buses city fleet (see Section 1.3.10) and Lothian Country Buses for services in West Lothian.

Above left (Image 254): Vehicle 1013/LXZ 5396 approaches the Hanover Street/ The Mound intersection of Princes Street on 5 May 2022 whilst working a Whitburn–Edinburgh Regent Road express service.

Above right (Image 255): Vehicle 1036/LXZ 5422 passes the Hanover Street/The Mound intersection of Princes Street on 21 August 2021 whilst working a Bathgate–Edinburgh Regent Road express service.

Left (Image 256): Vehicle 1044/ LXZ 5431 passes Princes Street Gardens on 12 April 2019 whilst working an Edinburgh Regent Road–Bathgate express service.

3.3.1.6: FLEET NUMBER 9201–9208
Volvo B8R with Plaxton Leopard Interurban bodywork
This fleet was delivered to Lothian Country Buses in April 2019 to operate a range of express services to Edinburgh Haymarket under the Green Arrow branding.

A brief interlude at Pinkhill on 19 July 2019 noted …

(Image 257): … vehicle 9204/SB19 GKJ working a Linlithgow–Edinburgh Haymarket express service.

(Image 258): … vehicle 9206/SB19 GKL working a Bathgate–Edinburgh Haymarket express service.

(Image 259): ... vehicle 9204/SB19 GKJ working an Edinburgh Haymarket–Bathgate express service.

(Image 260): Vehicle 9203/SB19 GKG pulls away from Haymarket Interchange on 4 March 2020 whilst working an Edinburgh Haymarket–Linlithgow express service.

SECTION 4:
LOTHIAN MOTORCOACHES

In the early 2000s, Lothian Buses closed down the coach business it had inherited in order to concentrate on stage coach and tour-bus services but in 2018 the company decided to return to the business by creating Lothian Motorcoaches and buying five Volvo B11RT tri-axle coaches with Plaxton Panther 3 bodywork (fleet numbers 9001–9005) and two Mercedes-Benz Sprinter mini-coaches in 2018 followed by six Volvo B11R two-axle coaches with Plaxton Panther 3 bodywork (fleet numbers 9006–9011) in 2019; the fleet was also enlarged by a variety of second-hand Volvo coaches. Note that the vehicles do not carry a fleet number on the external bodywork.

A brief interlude at the Hanover Street / The Mound intersection of Princes Street on 5 May 2022 noted …

(Image 261): … vehicle 9002/SN18 CVU approaching along Princes Street whilst operating a private hire tour.

(Image 262): … vehicle 9010/LC19 LMC, initially registered as SB19 GKY, approaching along Princes Street whilst operating a private hire tour. Note that this is one of the B11R two-axle coaches bought in 2019.

A brief interlude at the Hanover Street / The Mound intersection of Princes Street on 5 May 2022 noted …

(Image 263): …vehicle 9004/SN18 CVW crossing the Hanover Street/The Mound intersection of Princes Street whilst operating a private hire tour.

(Image 264): … vehicle 9002/SN18 CVU crossing the Hanover Street/The Mound intersection of Princes Street whilst operating a private hire tour.

SECTION 5: LOTHIAN TRAMWAYS

Lothian Tramways operated its first service on 31 May 2014 between Edinburgh Airport and York Place to mark the completion of Stage 1 of a proposed network that has its origins in the 1998 Edinburgh Airport Rail Link (EARL) project to improve services between Edinburgh Airport and the city centre. The inauguration of the service marked the end of a lengthy period of problems which had threatened the future of the scheme, with both political and financial problems causing delays to the construction. In the event, the intention of building a line from the airport, via Princes Street, to Newhaven was truncated to operate from the airport to a temporary terminus at York Place whilst the completion of the line to Newhaven was finally authorised in March 2019. In February 2022, services were truncated to St Andrews Square to allow the extension works to Newhaven to be undertaken, including the replacement of the York Place terminal by a new through halt at Picardy Place. As this album was being prepared, the service to Newhaven began operating during June 2023.

The operation of the line has changed from the initial New Edinburgh Tramways Company to Edinburgh Trams Ltd, a subsidiary of Transport for Edinburgh (TfE), that was created in 2010 to take over control. Since then TfE has also taken control of Lothian Buses to become the parent company of both the bus and tram operations. The tram vehicles are maintained at Gogar, on the city's western boundary, and although twenty-seven trams were ordered in 2007 and delivered during 2010, as at September 2022, only seventeen are required to provide the current daily service.

(Image 265): An unidentified tram calls at the tram stop adjacent to Princes Street Gardens on 10 April 2018 whilst working from York Place to the Airport.

Brief interludes at the Waverley Bridge junction with Princes Street during visits to Edinburgh have noted …

(Image 266): … Tram 251 passing Princes Street East Gardens on 31 July 2018 whilst working from York Place to the Airport.

(Image 267): … Tram 253 passing on 19 April 2017 whilst working from York Place to the Airport.

(Image 268): … Tram 257 passing on 19 April 2017 whilst working from York Place to the Airport.

(Image 269): Tram 265 weaves into Haymarket Interchange on 5 May 2022 whilst working from the Airport to St Andrews Square; the normal terminal point of York Place had been suspended to allow work to begin on the extension to Newhaven.

(Image 270): Tram 277, working from the Airport to St Andrews Square, meets Tram 272, working from St Andrews Square to the Airport, at Haymarket Interchange on 5 May 2022.

(Image 271): Tram 259 approaches Edinburgh Park Interchange on 31 July 2018 whilst working from York Place to the Airport.

Right (Image 272): Tram 275 approaches the Gyle Centre on 22 July 2016 whilst working from York Place to the Airport.

Below (Image 273): Tram 253, working from the Airport to York Place, departs from the Gyle Centre as Tram 269, working from York Place to the Airport, approaches the Gyle Centre on 22 July 2016.

(Image 274): Tram 270 prepares to cross the main Edinburgh Waverley–Glasgow Queen Street railway line at Carrick Knowe on 3 June 2015 whilst working from York Place to the Airport.